A Guide to Streaming Great Films

Elliott Kanbar

Also by Elliott Kanbar

You Finally Finished Your Film. Now What? (2013)

*Don't Let Your Film Die: How to Plan a Successful Launch
Without Going Broke* (2015)

The Tragedy of Moses (2016)

ELBAR Associates, LLC
P.O. Box 20038
New York, NY 10075

ISBN 978-0-578-41933-6
EAN 0-978-0-578-41933-6
Library of Congress Control Number: pdg

Printed in the United States of America

**Mack Sennett, Mabel Normand & Barney Oldfield,
"Barney Oldfield's Race for a Life"
June 3rd 1913**

Statistics & Facts

"U.S. consumers are more likely to stream entertainment from an internet service than tune in to live TV. Video-streaming services like Netflix have overtaken live programming as the viewing method of choice."
—Deloitte Digital Survey

"Revenue from traditional media (TV, cable TV, & DVDs) is falling and expected to continue falling through 2022. Meanwhile, revenue from streaming services (like Netflix, Amazon, and Hulu) is continuing its robust year-to-year growth." —The Hollywood Reporter

Netflix won 23 Emmys in 2018, tied with HBO.

"There are more streaming subscribers than traditional pay-TV customers in Britain, 15.4 million vs. 15.1 million."
—Stewart Clarke, Variety

"Broadcasters face more pressure than ever from declining ratings that are attributed to shifts toward digital viewing. The average percentage of people ages 18-34 watching television has declined from 16.1% to 10.5%."
—Daniel Holloway and Joe Otterson, Variety

"Seventy-eight percent of Facebook users watch live streaming on the platform." —Zero Gravity Marketing

"Among broadband-enabled households in the United States, 69% subscribe to at least one over-the-top (OTT) video service, while 38% subscribe to at least two. Households with three or more OTT subscriptions are the fastest growing category." —Parks Associates Research

"More than 168 million viewers accessed films on their smart phone in the last quarter of 2017. While traditional TV has far greater reach (292 million), a medium that barely existed 10

years ago now gets more video viewing than desktop or DVD viewing." —Variety.com

"Google Play is now selling movies in 117 countries, making it available in more markets than any transactional service in the world today." —Jonathan Zepp, Head of Worldwide Movie & TV Partnerships

A Definition

Streaming is the delivery of video or audio content directly to the viewing screen through the internet, bypassing cable or a satellite pay service.

It's a huge breakthrough in the world of entertainment, founded by engineers with enormous dedication, talent, and vision.

Lillian Gish "The Mothering Heart"
June 21st 1913

Contents

**Millie Liston & Matt Moore "Traffic in Souls"
November 24th 1913**

Introduction

> *"A film story must have a beginning, a middle, and an end*
> *. . . but not necessarily in that order."*
> —Jean-Luc Godard

It's incredible! We're in an unprecedented film lover's paradise thanks to a stupefying abundance of quality movies being streamed.

This is yet another gift from the digital revolution. Whether old or new films, whether made in the U.S.A., or coming from afar, quality viewing is landing nonstop in our homes and on our mobile devices.

Just read the following from a recent article by Erich Schwartzel in *The Wall Street Journal.*[1]

"Theater attendance last year [2017] fell to its lowest level since 1995, a crises propelled by the rise of streaming.. studios continue to shorten the amount of time a movie stays in theaters before becoming available at home, which threatens to push numbers down even more.. People have access to deep libraries of entertainment through [companies like] Netflix." By 2019, Netflix is expected to have 150 million subscribers.

There are seven major reasons why the streaming giants are causing so much concern in Hollywood.
1. They have big bucks to spend buying and making movies. They are now attending every major film festival and are often outbidding the major studios and distributors.

---

[1] "Comfiest Seat in the House: Struggling Movie Theaters Go Upscale to Survive" Erich Schwartzel, The Wall Street Journal, April 9, 2018, www.wsj.com/articles/comfiest-seat-in-the-house-struggling-movie-theaters-go-upscale-to-survive-1523285886.

2. Theater ticket prices are soaring with no end in sight. It's necessary because theater chains are incurring substantial debt to upgrade and modernize their auditoriums.

3. Streaming companies do not have to spend huge sums to advertise and market their films. They enjoy a built-in audience. Netflix has 130 million subscribers.

4. Advanced technology has produced superb flat screens, many with 4K and UHD (see chapter 1). As prices drop each year, these TVs may soon become more affordable to many families.

5. Home-viewing is simply more convenient. There are no traffic problems, you save on baby-sitters and parking, you can see the movie at your convenience, there are no worries about a basketball player sitting in front of you, there's no need to bundle up in winter, and you can watch the movie in your pajamas.

6. Streaming films at home offers attractive features not available in theaters: you can fast-forward, backtrack, play, pause and resume watching later on. And, for the hearing-impaired, most streamed films, even the ones in English, offer closed-captioning.

7. Streaming allows you to binge. If you're hooked on a series, you can simply watch episode after episode in one sitting.

For cinephiles, these developments are phenomenal. In today's technology-driven world, the multitude of available films has overwhelmed most people, even the savvy technocrats and young geeks. Which are the films worth watching? Where can these films be accessed?

Glenn Kenny wrote the following in *The New York Times*:[2] "It's no secret that Netflix doesn't do a good job letting consumers know the recent critical favorites that are available. So, if you're on that site and looking for hidden gems, you're not going to find them gathered under a category. Nor is it a sure thing that the algorithm is going to recommend suitable films to you."

In the not so distant past, "films" was the common parlance and people knew what you meant. But now, the TV and movie viewing world has exploded, with thousands of high quality digital video options to choose from. With terms like streaming, platforms, OTT, TV sticks, back-lighting and quantum dots, life got a lot more complicated.

But help is here. This guide's first four chapters will cover the equipment needed to maximize the viewing experience. Next will be a rundown of the many diverse platforms (such as Netflix, Amazon, iTunes) and the types of content they offer. Also included are helpful hints, recommended subscriptions and books, and a comprehensive glossary.

This guide also speaks plain English and plain truths. Our goal is to impart information that the average consumer can understand. And our opinions are totally above board. We accept no kick backs or fees for any recommendations we make.

So, pull up a seat and enjoy a world of blissful entertainment.

---

[2] "The Hidden Gems of 2017 Movies Are on . . . Netflix?" Glenn Kenny, The New York Times, January 19, 2018, www.nytimes.com/2018/01/19/movies/hidden-gems-2017-movies-netflix.html.

King Baggot & Herbert Brenon "Ivanhoe"
September 22nd 1913

Step #1. Buying the Right TV

"The only safe thing is to take a chance."
—Mike Nichols

The TV you buy is going to be your most important purchase when it comes to streaming films at home. The choices can be overwhelming. Just visit the TV section at Costco, Walmart, or Best Buy and the experience will surely trigger vertigo.

Tips Before Buying a TV

1. Select the largest TV that will fit your room and your budget. The extra cost will be worth it. Buying the largest possible TV screen will offer you a thrilling theatrical experience. TV screens are measured diagonally.

2. For the best picture quality at a reasonable cost, go with 4K UHD. It offers eight megapixels of resolution instead of the two megapixels in the HDTV. You'll get a far brighter picture, but be aware of the following: the TV set will be more expensive, fewer films will be available, and some platforms, like Netflix, will charge more to upgrade to this level.

3. Check out our glossary to familiarize yourself with a few technical TV terms.

4. Select 120 Hz over 60 Hz. This refers to the frame rate. At 120Hz, the TV picture will be faster and less blurry, which is particularly important when viewing action films and sporting events.

5. Most TVs use LCD display panels with LED backlighting. Some techies prefer the LG brand's

OLED. Samsung's QLED offers enhanced LCD and competes favorably with LG's OLED.

6. Buy a smart TV. This will make it easier to access the major platforms like Netflix, Amazon, iTunes, and Hulu. Also, a smart TV will probably not need a separate media streamer (See chapter 3).

7. List the important features you'll want in your TV. Unless you're going to be using multiple apps, a less expensive TV can usually do the job.

8. Invest in a universal remote control. With this one unit, you'll be able to access your Blu-ray player, cable or satellite box, and other devices connected to your TV.

9. Buy a sound bar. Flat TVs are too thin to project good sound quality. A sound bar will bring you closer to that great theatrical experience when streaming films (See chapter 2).

10. Before browsing for a TV, you'll come across a few unfamiliar brands offering substantially lower prices than the competition. Most lack competent customer service people, some use inferior parts, and you'll probably have to pay a hefty delivery charge. In this guide, we'll list only the top-tier brand name TV manufacturers.

11. When shopping for a TV, zero in on one specific model for the purpose of comparison. Then compare prices for that model in a variety of major stores and online outlets. Even if you later decide to switch to a different model, the store that offered you the lowest price for the comparison model will probably offer the lowest price for the final choice model.

12. Before buying a warranty from the store, check with your credit card company. They may offer protection at no cost. Also check the length of the warranty and read the fine print.

13. Opt for an HDR set that is compatible with Dolby Vision, a video format used in many theaters and now available on many movies for home viewing. It will produce more realistic colors and better contrast.

14. Curved TVs sound exciting, but they do not improve picture quality and will not work if there are multiple viewers sitting in different locations.

15. You will not regret buying a TV with a minimum of four HDMI inputs and two USB ports.

16. Timing is crucial in buying a TV. New models are introduced in the spring, so expect higher prices at that time. They then start to drop and reach low levels by October 01. Best deals can be found after Thanksgiving and after Christmas.

The Best-Rated TVs:

We checked three rating services: Consumer Reports (consumerreports.org), Tom's Guide (tomsguide.com), and Best Products (bestproducts.com). Each did extensive testing of the models and, we sensed they were objective. We limited our lists to TVs selling between $400 and $3,000 and not larger than sixty-five inches or smaller than forty inches. Prices listed are for purposes of general comparison at time of printing and are subject to change.
All TVs listed are 4K UHD.

Consumer Reports

Sixty-Five Inch Screen

- **LG OLED 65C7P. Active HDR with Dolby Vision.** $2,500. Wi-Fi capable, 120Hz refresh rate, 2160p resolution, and includes four HDMI inputs and three USB ports.

- **LG 65SJ8000. Active HDR with Dolby Stereo.** $1,235. Wi-Fi capable, 240Hz refresh rate, 2160p resolution, and includes four HDMI inputs and three USB ports.

- **Samsung UN65MU650D.** $950. Wi-Fi capable, 2160p resolution, 120Hz refresh rate, and includes three HDMI inputs and two USB ports.

Fifty-Five Inch Screen

- **LG OLED55C8PUA. Active HDR with Dolby Stereo.** $2,500. Wi-Fi capable, 2160p resolution, and includes four HDMI inputs and three USB ports.

- **Samsung UN55NU8000.** $900. Wi-Fi capable, 2160p resolution, 240Hz refresh rate, and includes four HDMI inputs and two USB ports.

- **TCL 55P607.** $650. Wi-Fi capable, 2160p resolution, 120Hz refresh rate, and includes three HDMI inputs and one USB port.

Forty-Nine Inch Screen

- **Samsung UN49MU6500.** $750. Wi-Fi capable, 2160p resolution, 120 Hz refresh rate, and includes three HDMI inputs and two USB ports.

Forty-Inch Screen

- **Samsung UN40MU6300.** $400. Wi-Fi capable, 2160p resolution, 120Hz refresh rate, and includes three HDMI inputs and two USB ports.

Tom's Guide

Tom's Guide rates TVs in three categories. Here are the preferred TVs in each category.

- **Best value: Fifty-five inch TCL 55P607 with Roku's smart TV interface.** $649. It offers robust HDR support with compatibility for both HDR10 and Dolby Vision.

- **Best TV under $700: Fifty-five inch Samsung MU6300 with HDR10.** $599. An UHD Smart LED TV, Wi-Fi capable, 1080p resolution, and includes three HDMI inputs and two USB ports.

- **Best picture quality: Fifty-five inch Sony Bravia OLED X BR-55A1A.** $2,498. An OLED UHD TV, Wi-Fi capable, 2160p resolution, and includes four HDMI inputs and three USB ports.

Best Products

- **Sixty-five inch Sony XBR X850E.** $1,300. 4K HDR Smart Android TV with Sony's excellent X1 picture processing system, and includes four HDMI inputs and three USB ports.

- **Fifty-five inch LG OLED 55C7P with active HDR and Dolby Vision.** $1,900. Smart TV, exceptional OLED picture, and includes four HDMI inputs and three USB ports.

- **Forty-nine inch Samsung MU7500.** $878. One of the most affordable 4K curved smart televisions on the market, and includes three HDMI inputs, and an Ethernet port.

Conclusion

For the average viewer, most of these TVs listed above will provide an excellent picture. Prices will vary based on the size of the TV, the features offered, and where you make your purchase. The race to be the first country to offer 5G is heating up. That will open up more options in buying the right TV.

2

Step #2. Buying the Right Sound Bar

"The only time success comes before work is in the dictionary."

—Samuel Goldwyn

Having a large flat-screen TV without a sound bar is like having a martini without an olive.

Here's an excerpt from *Consumer Reports.*

> As TVs slim down, the quality of their sound often follows suit. The reason is fairly simple: there's less room for a powerful sound system. Perfectly adequate for routine programming—sitcoms, reality shows, talk shows, and the like—but for movies and even TV dramas, you might want richer, fuller sound. To compensate, get a sound bar speaker, an easier and less expensive fix than purchasing a complete add-on component system.[3]

A forty-inch sound bar can be mounted on the wall or placed above or below the TV. If space is limited, you can consider a sound base. This unit will sit on a stand or table under the TV.

With most sound bars, you'll get two speakers and a separate subwoofer (2.1 channel sound setup). A good sound bar is a cost-effective way to upgrade your TV and to produce a theater-like experience when streaming films.

Here are some tips for buying a sound bar.

1. In most cases, a sound bar with 2.1 channels (two front channels and a separate subwoofer) should be

---

[1] "Sound Bar Buying Guide: Raising the Bar," Consumer Reports, June 2018, www.consumerreports.org/cro/sound-bars/buying-guide/index.htm.

enough. If you want true surround sound, buy a sound bar with a subwoofer and rear speakers—preferably wireless—for multichannel sound.

2. Consider placement. If you'll be placing the sound bar on the TV stand, make sure there's enough room in front of the TV and that it isn't so tall that it will block the remote control beam.

3. Don't overbuy. If you're using the sound bar only for watching films on TV, you can opt for a lower priced, no-frills model.

4. Make sure the types of inputs on the sound bar match the types of outputs on the source components.

5. Try them out. Major stores will allow you to listen to different sound bars before you purchase. Ask about their policy for returns and exchanges.

6. Check the warranty, including the length, and the conditions. Before buying an extended warranty, check with your credit card company. They may offer protection at no cost.

7. Sound bars often have less power and fewer options than a traditional sound system, so they are not the best choice in a very large room or auditorium.

Here's a rundown of the best sound bars from a few well-regarded testing companies: *Consumer Reports* (consumerreports.org), *Tom's Guide* (tomsguide.com), *Consumer Search* (consumersearch.com), and *Digital Trends* (digitaltrends.com). Prices subject to change.

Consumer Reports

- **Sonos Playbar.** $700. Best Choice. Comes with 5.1 channels and one speaker. It can be combined with other Sonos speakers to become part of a multi room setup. It can also be used as the front-channel speaker in a multichannel surround system in one room.

- **LG SH7B.** $400. Comes with 3.1 channels and 1.1 speakers. Houses both front and side firing speakers and can connect to your home network using the Ethernet or a Wi-Fi connection. It also comes with a wireless subwoofer and Bluetooth.

- **Samsung HW-K550.** $370. Comes with 3.1 channels and six built-in speakers, each designed with a dedicated amplifier. It has a wireless subwoofer. The speaker has Bluetooth with NFC for easy pairing with mobile devices and two HDMI inputs.

Tom's Guide

- **Sonos Playbase. Best Choice.** $700. The Playbase is big on bass and offers rich vocals thanks to its ten custom-made drivers. It does a great job doubling as a Wi-Fi speaker, and it can be paired with other Sonos speakers. It also supports voice commands via Amazon's Alexa. Caveat: make sure there is enough room to accommodate the TV on the top.

- **Polk Magnifi Mini.** $220. Comes with a 2.1 channel sound bar with a wireless subwoofer. It has Bluetooth, Wi-Fi, and a built-in Google Chromecast.

- **Sony HT-ST5000.** $1,500. A 7.1.2-channel system with a wireless subwoofer. It can decode Dolby Digital and DTS and has Atmos compatibility, making this Sony a superb sound bar. It also features Bluetooth with NFC for easy connection with other devices.

- **JBL Cinema.** $450 to $499. Optimized for UHD TVs and offers 4K pass-through to preserve the full audio quality of 4K content. Includes a subwoofer.

Consumer Search

- **Yamaha YAS-203. Best value.** $449. Has six speakers and a 6.25-inch wireless subwoofer. Devices connect via Bluetooth. Its HDMI connections support 4K and an HDR pass-through.

- **Sonos Playbar. Best high-end.** $700. See the first Tom's Guide entry.

Digital Trends

- **Samsung HW-K950. Best choice.** $1,200. Includes a powerful Dolby Atmos surround sound in a simple package. It also comes with wireless satellite speakers for true surround sound immersion.

- **Samsung HW-MS650.** $430. The MS650 delivers a 3.0 channel configuration (left, right, center) via a combination of six woofers and three tweeters, to produce exceptional sound for the money.

- **Vizio SB3621. Best value.** $148. The best sound bar under $200. It can decode basic DTS and Dolby formats and offers an easy connection for your components via Bluetooth. A wireless subwoofer is also included.

Additional option: Recently introduced is the Sonos Beam for $399. It's powered by Amazon's Alexa offering hands-free controls. Excellent unit for the price.

Improved Sound for Those with Hearing Loss

Many with some degree of hearing loss have a hard time watching TV. Even after turning up the volume, it's hard for them to make out the dialogue. Sound bars are a partial solution. Here are a few more.

1. Transmitting the audio directly to the hearing aids. An audiologist can set this up if you have the right kind of hearing aids.

2. Closed-captioning. Most films today, including English-speaking films, include this option.

3. Some TVs include two-way Bluetooth that allows sound to be transmitted directly to wireless headphones.

Conclusion
No doubt! The sound from your TV will be substantially enhanced with a sound bar or sound base.

**Mabel Normand "Mabel at the Wheel"
April 18th 1914**

3
Step#3. Buying the Right Media Streamer

"I made mistakes in drama. I thought drama was when actors cried. But drama is when the audience cries."
—Frank Capra

A media streamer will allow you to stream films from internet outlets like Netflix, Amazon, iTunes, and Hulu directly to your TV.

Most of the smart 4K TVs now sold and listed in chapter 1 have a built-in media streamer. If you own an older TV, you should purchase a media streamer to watch films from the most popular platforms. In effect, a media streamer will convert your old TV into a smart TV.

If you own a 4K TV with a built-in media streamer, is it necessary to buy an additional one?

To answer that question, consider the following:

- The add-on media streamer may often outperform and/or be easier to use than the built-in streamer.

- It can serve as a good backup.

- It can include platforms that are not available on your smart TV. For many years, Apple TV did not include the Amazon platform. To watch a film on Amazon Prime, you would have needed an additional media streamer. If you're a fan of iTunes, then you'll need the Apple TV media streamer. As of now, iTunes is not available anywhere else.

- A media streamer may offer more content. Some can transmit a lineup of podcasts on many subjects including news, sports, technology, learning languages, cooking, and comedy.

- It is easy to install. Just plug the unit into your TV and then connect it to your wireless network.

- It is inexpensive. See the prices below.

- All streaming media devices have built-in Wi-Fi.

In a recent survey of smart TV owners, *Consumer Reports* found that 60 percent of the respondents ended up using an external media streamer in addition to the TV's built-in system.[4]

Barb Gonzalez, writing for *Lifewire*, offers the following tips about buying a media streamer:[5]

1. Be sure it will play the file formats of the media you own. Most players will list the media file formats that it is capable of playing on the box.

2. Make sure it will produce the best picture for your TV. Whether you have an older picture-tube TV or a 4K HDTV, the media player you choose should be compatible with the TV to ensure a quality picture.

---

[4] "Best 4K Streaming Media Devices," James K. Willcox, Consumer Reports, February 23, 2018, www.consumerreports.org/streaming-media-devices/best-4k-streaming-media-devices/.

[5] "How to Shop for a Network Media Player or Media Streamer," Barb Gonzalez, Lifewire, August 4, 2017, www.Lifewire.com/shop-for-a-network-media-player-1847438.

3. Decide which content you want. The media streamer you select should be able to transmit the platforms you watch most frequently.

4. If you also want to listen to music, view photos, and connect to social networking sites, select a media streamer that will offer these options.

5. If you want to save films for later viewing, select a media streamer with a hard drive.

6. Make sure it has a USB connection. This will allow you to play media from a connected camera, camcorder, external hard drive, or flash drive.

7. If the player can stream media from your smartphone or tablet device, then you'll be able to film an event outside your home on your cell phone or tablet and stream it on your TV when you come home.

Here's a review of the most highly rated media streamers now available. For 4K streaming, the market is dominated in alphabetical order, by Amazon Fire TV, Apple TV, Google Chromecast, and Roku. Some of these devices are set-top models; others plug directly into a TV's HDMI slot. Most also support HDR technology.

Amazon Fire TV with 4K UHD and Alexa Voice Remote. $70. "It's a diamond-shaped dongle with HDR capability, and support for a smooth-looking 60-frames-per-second video. It also supports Dolby Atmos surround video and the HDR10 format. Surprisingly, it does not support Dolby Vision. But Fire's most attractive feature may be the Alexa Voice remote which can find, launch, and control content by voice. Main drawback is fewer services than some of its competitors as it prioritizes Amazon content." (James K. Willcox, *Consumer Reports*)[6]

---

[6] "Best 4K Streaming Media Devices," James K. Willcox.

"If you're an Amazon Prime member, there's no better streaming device that rewards you like the Fire TV Stick." (David Beren, *Lifewire*)[7]

Apple TV 4K. $180 for the 32 GB version and $200 for the 64 GB version. "Includes a Siri voice assistant and updated touchpad remote. It also supports both HDR10 and Dolby Vision HDR formats. Best deals for those watching iTunes most frequently." (James K. Willcox, *Consumer Reports*)[8] …"With the inclusion of the A10XFusion chip, the Apple TV 4K has twice the processing power—and four times the graphics performance—of its predecessor. The Apple TV 4K is the only streaming device you need." (Stefan Vazharov, Best Products.com)[9]

Google Chromecast Ultra. $70. "Includes a 4K HDR Streamer. No remote control. Instead, you use the Google Home app on your smartphone or tablet to find content. A drawback is that it takes a couple of extra steps to play Amazon videos. Supports Dolby Vision HDR. The Chromecast Ultra has a dual-band WiFi for connecting to a home network and an Ethernet port on the power adapter for a more reliable connection." (James K. Willcox, *Consumer Reports*)[10]…."Major flaw is the lack of iTunes and Amazon content." (David Berens, *Lifewire*)[11]

Roku Streaming Stick and Roku Ultra. $70 for the Roku Stick and $100 for the Roku ULTRA. "If you want a 4K HDR Roku player but don't want a visible set-top box, then this

---

[7] "The 10 Best Devices to Buy in 2018 for Streaming TV," David Beren, *Lifewire*, August 6, 2018, www.*Lifewire*.com/best-devices-to-buy-for-streaming-tv-4061016.

[8] "Best 4K Streaming Media Devices," James K. Willcox.

[9] "The Apple TV 4K Is the Only Streaming Device You Need," Stefan Vazharov, bestproducts.com, September 21, 2017, www.bestproducts.com/tech/electronics/a1753/apple-tv-4k-review/.

[10] "Best 4K Streaming Media Devices," James K. Willcox, *Consumer Reports*.

[11] "The 10 Best Devices to Buy in 2018 for Streaming TV" David Beren, *Lifewire*.

stick-style player is a best choice. The Roku ULTRA offers great performance and a wide assortment of channels (5,000 and counting). The Roku ULTRA also has a button on the unit that causes a misplaced remote to beep, and a headphone jack in the remote control for private listening." (James K. Willcox, *Consumer Reports*)[12]…"The Roku ULTRA is the best overall media streamer." (David Berens, *Lifewire*)[13]

Special bonus: Roku now offers its own streaming channel featuring popular movies and TV shows (See chapter 4).

Conclusion
If you're an avid film buff and prepared to pay the price, the Apple TV is your best bet. It offers iTunes, which is a big plus. If you have other Apple devices, you can use AirPlay to stream from these devices directly to your Apple TV. The Apple TV comes with the A10X Fusion, one of the most powerful chipsets around. It easily delivers UHD video and improves content resolution.

---

[12] "Best 4K Streaming Media Devices," James K. Willcox, *Consumer Reports*.

[13] "The 10 Best Devices to Buy in 2018 for Streaming TV," David Beren, *Lifewire*.

Charlie Chaplin "A Night Out"
February 15th 1915

4
Step#4. Buying the Right Router and Modem

"We don't make movies to make money; we make money to make movies."

—Walt Disney

Most people watching movies on a TV are unaware of the importance of having an effective and efficient router and modem. One reason is that the workings of a router and modem are beyond the comprehension of the average person. These units are too technical, too complicated. But having the right router and modem is essential in producing an optimum picture.

Here's an overview.

The Router

The router is a unit that distributes information coming from the internet to all the devices located in a house, apartment, or office. So if you're watching a movie on the TV in your den, and your kid is playing a video game in his bedroom, and your spouse is using a computer in the kitchen, the router does the job of distributing information quickly and accurately to each device being used.

A wireless router is recommended. *Consumer Reports* listed the following reasons:[14]

- If you are often moving around your house, apartment, or office using a laptop or other mobile device, you're better off with a wireless connection.

- Wireless eliminates the clutter of having multiple cables.

---

[14] "Wireless Router Buying Guide," Consumer Reports, October 2017, www.consumerreports.org/cro/wireless-routers/buying-guide/index.htm.

- It's more economical to own your own router than to rent one from your internet service provider.

- You may have a broadband modem directly connected to a single computer, but you want to have connections with multiple devices.

- Your current router has only wired connectivity, but you want to go online with wireless devices.

- Your existing router is too slow or its wireless range is too short to reach important places in your home.

- You can choose the router you want.

Purchasing a Router

If you live in a small apartment, then a basic, inexpensive router should do the job. A more powerful router will be needed in larger apartments, houses and offices with multiple floors and rooms.

For best results, purchase a dual-band router. One connects to the 2.4 GHz band and the other to the 5 GHz band. You'll have minimal signal interference making it ideal for video streaming. Also, request the more advanced 802.11ac router for more power and best results.

Recommendations (prices subject to change).

- **Netgear R7000.** $180. This unit has a 1 GHz dual-core processor and can meet multiple, simultaneous demands, even in larger apartments, houses, or offices.

- **D-Link DIR-866L.** $160. This is an advanced router at a reasonable price.

- **TREDnet TEW-812DRU AC1750.** $136. An affordable router with good performance.

- **TP-Link AC1750.** $76. A dual-band gigabit wireless router that can stream in 4K at a really low price. Excellent in small spaces.

- **Apple AirPort Extreme Base Station.** $99. This is the best router for households with Apple TV and other Apple devices.

Modems

Unfortunately, you can't connect your network of devices directly to the internet with just the router. The router must be connected to a modem in order to transmit digital traffic. As stated earlier, a router distributes information coming from the internet to all of the devices in your house, apartment, or office. A modem connects that network—and thus all the devices connected to the router—to the internet.

In many cases, the internet service provider offers a modem at a monthly rental price between $8 to $15. As with a router, it's more economical to buy your own modem.

Recommendations (prices subject to change).

- **Netgear CM600.** $89.99.

- **Motorola MB7621.** $84.99

- **TP-Link TC7650.** $79.99.

Dual Router/Modem Units

A router/modem combo saves space, has fewer wires, and probably costs less compared to buying these units separately. A disadvantage is that if either the router or the modem conks out, you'll have to buy another complete combo unit.

Recommendations (prices subject to change).

- **TP-Link Archer CR700.** $110.99.

- **Linksys AC1600.** $110.00.

- **Netgear N600.** $99.49.

Mesh Networks

Black spots (sometimes called dead zones) prevent your router from reaching certain areas of your home or office. The building materials used and/or the surrounding landscapes may cause this. A solution may be to purchase a mesh network router. Two recommendations are the Nova Whole Home Mesh Wi-Fi System ($300) or the less expensive TP-Link Archer C9 ($145.83).

A Note about Security

Routers are the most frequently exploited devices by hackers. Some of the newer routers include built-in security software. The most obvious remedies are using stronger passwords, turning off the features you are not using, and installing antivirus software.

Conclusion
The size of your room and the size and power of your TV should determine the type of router and modem you should purchase. They can be costly, but getting the best models can considerably enhance the picture on your TV screen, and discourage hacking.

W.C. Fields "Pool Sharks"
September 19th 1915

Chapter 5
Streaming Films On Your Cell Phone and Laptop

"The end of a film is always an end of a life."
—Sam Peckinpah

Watching a film on a cell phone or laptop is becoming very popular. And for good reason. While these devices cannot replicate the dramatic impact of watching a film on a flatscreen TV, they do offer many advantages: you can watch films almost anywhere you go, on a train or bus, on the beach, in a park, or even while strolling around town. And, it's often far simpler to access a film on a cell phone or laptop than on a TV.

Understandably, most people do not select a cell phone or laptop for its excellence in streaming films. You should also be aware that not all cell phones and laptops are suitable for streaming films.

Ideally, it's best to select a cell phone or laptop that will handle all your needs including streaming films.

Cell Phones.

Streaming films on cell phones can be tricky. Make sure the cell phone you buy can access your favorite platforms. You'll then be able to consider it as your mini-TV.

Jon Knight in *Gadget Hacks*[15] ranked the best cell phones for streaming films. Prices subject to change.

#1. **ROG Phone.** $899.00. Primarily known as a gaming phone, they now can stream films.

---

[15]"Compare Phones", Jon Knight *GadgetHacks.com*
www.gadgethacks.com/compare/

#2. **Galaxy Note 9.** $999.00. This new model has an improved display, bigger battery, and better speakers.

#3. **iPhone Xs Max.** $1,099.00. Offers a large display in a small footprint with a high resolution.

#4. **LG V40 ThinQ.** $999.00. LG introduced new phone speakers known as Boombox that use a resonance chamber to amplify the sound.

#5. **Google Pixel 3 XL**. $899.00. The standout feature is its front-facing stereo speakers.

The most popular platforms for streaming films on a cell phone are Netflix, Amazon Prime, Hulu, and HBO Now.

Laptops.

Obviously, laptops come with a larger screen than a cell phone for viewing films. They also offer more accessories such as Bluetooth speakers, a DVD or CD drive, and a hard drive for storing films.

Here are three laptops that are particularly suitable for streaming films:

#1. **Apple MacBook Pro.** $1,199. 13.3" screen. Has a good amount of charge allowing you to binge for up to 7 hours.

#2. **Dell XPS 13.** $999. 13.3" screen. Offers a high definition screen.

#3. **Asus VivoBook F51OUA.** $595.00. 14.2" screen. A larger screen at a reasonable price.

Another Option. If you want a separate laptop just for streaming films and nothing else, you might consider these inexpensive models: Acer Chromebook CB3-131-C3SZ ($229.00), Toshiba Chromebook 2 ($275.00), or the Asus VivoBook E403SA-US21 ($390).

Conclusion

If you're planning to stream films on your cell phone or lap top, make sure the unit you buy has this capability. And, of course, as new units come on the market, they may be preferable to the ones mentioned in this chapter.

**Mary Pickford & Marshall Neilan "The Sheik"
November 7ʰ 1915**

6
Transactional Video on Demand (TVOD) Platforms

"Drama is life with the dull bits cut out."
—Alfred Hitchcock

If you are selecting a film from a transactional platform, you will pay for each film you view. However, you will not be obligated to subscribe and commit to paying a monthly or annual subscription fee.

Renting a film will vary, but it should average between $2 and $5 per film. Another option is to purchase the movie. That cost would average between $15 and $20.

Generally, with some exceptions, you have thirty days to start watching a movie after you rent it. After you start watching the movie, you have forty-eight hours to finish it. You can watch the movie as often as you like during the thirty-day period. If you do not watch a movie within the thirty-day period, you'll have to rent it again.

There are three major benefits to accessing a film on a transactional platform.

1. If you don't expect to watch many films during the course of a year, it will probably cost less than going with a subscription.

2. Transactional platforms may offer more content.

3. A transactional platform will often have a film that a subscription platform does not have.

There are many transactional platforms out there. Here are some very popular ones (prices subject to change).

- **iTunes** (apple.com/itunes/video.com). The rental fee for a new movie runs around $5 for Standard

Definition (SD) and $6 for High Definition (HD). Purchasing a film costs around $15 for SD and $20 for HD. Older movies are available at a lower cost. "iTunes continues to have the biggest catalog of music and video offerings—more than 28 million songs and 45,000 films, and 85,000 TV episodes. Most notably missing is support for streaming purchased content to iOS devices. If you plan to buy or rent a film on your iPhone, iPad, or iPod Touch, you must download to play it, and that can take some time. Only Apple TV lets you stream iTunes instantly." (pcworld.com).[16] Available on the following devices: Mac, Apple TV, iPhone, iPad and iPod touch. Watch for occasional sales, sometimes offering film rentals for only ninety-nine cents.

- **Amazon Instant Video** (amazon.com). Most Amazon films costs less than iTunes. Rentals can run as low as ninety-nine cents for some films and rarely go higher than $5. "Amazon films can be streamed on the iPad, Xbox 360, PlayStation 3, Roku, and many other home video TV products. This gives Amazon a clear advantage over iTunes." (cnet.com)[17]
On the other hand, and this may change, iTunes offers more content. Currently Amazon is focusing on buying completed films rather than investing in original programming. If you are a subscriber to the Amazon shopping service, you can subscribe to Amazon Instant Video at no extra charge.

- **Vudu** (vudu.com). Vudu charges less than iTunes and a bit more than Amazon. Films are generally

---

[16] "Google Play vs. Amazon vs. iTunes Store: How the Content Stores Stack Up," Yardena Arar, PCWorld, July 10, 2012, www.pcworld.com/article/259040/google_play_vs_amazon_vs_itunes_store_h ow_the_content_stores_stack_up.html.
[17] "Amazon Instant Video Review," Jason Parker, CNET, August 3, 2012, www.cnet.com/reviews/amazon-instant-video-review/.

$1.99 for Standard Definition (SD) and $2.99 for High Definition (HD). Since being acquired by Walmart, its library has expanded considerably. They offer a five-star rating system and a Rotten Tomatoes score for most films. There is no opportunity for offline viewing. When you order an episode, it is not downloaded to your device. Instead, it streams using your broadband connection on devices such as PlayStation 3 and 4, Blu-ray, HD televisions, and Apple iOS devices. Rentals can be charged to your Walmart account.

- **Fandango Now** (fandangonow.com). Rentals are around $5 a film, but the company offers reward points that can reduce the cost of future rentals. Each SD TV episode costs $2.99. An attractive feature is that they now offer many films that recently completed theatrical runs. The major drawbacks are frequent glitches, and it doesn't work with some popular devices. Fandango Now currently works on Samsung, Vizio, LQ smart TVs, Roku, and Chromecast. It doesn't work on Apple TV, Xbox, or PlayStation. To date, it doesn't offer original programming of films or parental controls.

- **Google Play** (play.google.com/movies). Standard cost is $1.99 per film. Google Play highlights popular shows and movies from both network TV and cable channels. Currently there are limited HD options. The best way to watch content on this platform is to use Chromecast. Without that add-on, you can stream only the shows on your computer or Android smartphone and tablet. To date, it doesn't offer original programming of films. Google Play is best if you want to catch a missed TV show or series.

- **Redbox on Demand** (redbox.com/ondemand). In keeping with its base of budget-wise, convenience-seeking customers, Redbox decided that this new service will charge customers only when a film is viewed. It will also keep its rates low: $2 for older films, $4 for new releases, and $10 to purchase. Redbox only recently started their streaming service, so it will take them some time to catch up to the competition. However, Redbox is supported by a few major devices like Apple TV, Roku, Android, and iOS.

- **Paramount Movies** (paramountmovies.com). SD films are $4.99, HD films are $5.99. To purchase a film it's $14.99. Available are many Paramount films, CBS Theatrical films, DreamWorks animation, and selected films from PBS and BBC. Films can be streamed on the PC, Mac, iPhone, iPad, Android smartphones and tablets, and Xbox.

Conclusion

These sites are attractive for those who do not plan to see many movies during the course of the year. Also, there might be films you are interested in seeing that are offered on these sites, that are not available on the subscription platforms.

7

Subscription Video on Demand (SVOD) Platforms

"If a million people see my movie, I hope they see a million different movies."

—Quentin Tarantino

The incredible success of these platforms has given Hollywood execs and major film distributors big-time headaches. And for good reason: with an SVOD platform, a subscriber can access an unlimited number of films for one set price each month. What's worrisome to Hollywood is that the streaming companies are buying and producing films of the highest quality. Netflix, the current leader, has 130 million subscribers worldwide and expects to spend $9 billion in 2019 on producing original content.

SVOD is the future of the film business. In time, every major Hollywood studio will have a streaming outlet.

Here are the major players. Again, prices are subject to change.

- **Netflix** (netflix.com). $8 per month for Standard Definition (SD) on a single screen; $11 per month for High Definition (HD) up to two screens; $14 per month for 4K Ultra High Definition (UHD), up to four screens. Netflix offers the greatest range of major studio films and revivals. Most impressively, they are investing heavily in original programming. Netflix is available on almost every kind of streaming device and includes closed-captioning on all films. A disadvantage is that, unlike Hulu and Amazon, Netflix is usually a year behind in streaming TV episodes.

- **Amazon Prime** (amazon.com/prime). $119 per year or $12.99 per month. Check for student discounts. Amazon Prime includes the Amazon shopping benefits of free shipping of goods and two-day delivery, Amazon Photo, Kindle Lending Library, and Amazon Music. Amazon Prime is making an aggressive move to acquire more film products and to compete with Netflix. However, they are still far behind when it comes to high-end original programming. Amazon Prime has an edge over Netflix in that there is no extra cost for 4K UHD content with HDR. It has become more kid friendly with its exclusive deal with Nickelodeon, MTV, and Comedy Central. It is available on most streaming devices except Chromecast. Amazon Prime can be streamed on most smart TVs, PlayStation 3 and 4, Xbox 360, Xbox One, Wii, WiiU, iPhone, iPad, Roku, Amazon Fire TV, and Android phones.

- **Hulu Plus** (hulu.com). $7.99 per month (with commercials) or $12 per month (no commercials). It has discontinued its free ad-supported platform. It's popular with viewers interested in TV programs and popular TV series. The movie selection is small but growing rapidly. Its big break came with the success of *"The Handmaid's Tale"*, which won an Emmy. Two major drawbacks are that it offers only a select number of episodes from some TV series, and it does not offer streaming from every major TV network.

- **HBO NOW** (hbonow.com) and **HBO GO** (hbogo.com). HBO NOW is $14.99 per month. If you are already an HBO cable subscriber, then you can get HBO GO at no additional cost. HBO GO offers the same programs and services as HBO NOW. With HBO NOW you'll get decades of popular HBO films, documentaries, and events. You can also get most of your favorite HBO series. However, the movie selection is minimal, which may be a drawback, depending on your viewing interests. Also, HBO NOW does not allow offline viewing. It's now available on the following devices: Amazon Fire TV, Apple TV,

Chromecast, Xbox, Roku, Samsung, and PlayStation Vue.

- **FilmStruck** (filmstruck.com). $7 per month for the basic service; $11 per month or $99 per year with the Criterion Channel. This is the go-to platform for film lovers of independent art house and classic movies. FilmStruck is a joint venture with Turner Classic Movies and the Criterion Collection. They offer access to the entire Janus library and hundreds of classic movies from Warner Bros.

- **Acorn TV** (support.acorn.tv). $5 per month or $50 per year. Acorn offers excellent European comedies, dramas, and mysteries, including films by Agatha Christie as well as the comedy series *"Alfresco"*. Available devices are Roku, Amazon Fire TV and Amazon Fire TV Stick, Apple TV, iPhone and iPad, Android, and Chromecast. Currently Acorn TV is available only in the United States, the US Virgin Islands, Marshall Islands, American Samoa, Guam, Puerto Rico, and parts of Canada.

- **MUBI** (mubi.com). $9 per month. MUBI offers a unique model of introducing a new film each day and making each film available for thirty days. MUBI searches for festival films that were unable to find a distributor as well as films from lesser known filmmakers. It also partners with the Criterion Collection, Celluloid Dreams, and Martin Scorsese's World Cinema Foundation. Available on the following devices: Chromecast, Apple TV, PlayStation 3 and 4, Amazon Fire TV, and smart TVs.

- **Fandor** (fandor.com). $4.99 per month. Fandor now offers more than 5,000 films focusing mostly on independent and foreign features. According to Gail Gendler, the company's head of programming,

Fandor seeks to acquire films that "the big players don't think are worth acquiring."

- **Showtime Anytime** (showtime.com). $11 per month. Following its rival HBO, Showtime, the cable outlet, has formed a streaming platform. For starters, past Showtime productions, movies, documentaries, and sporting events will be available on the streaming platform. The service is currently available only on Apple devices, but more are to follow.

- **CBS All Access** (cbs.com/all-access). $5.99 per month with advertising and $9.99 per month with no advertising. Launched in 2014, it became the first over-the-top service offered by an American broadcast television network. The site allows subscribers to view past and present CBS shows. In 2016, the site received approval to stream selected NFL games, and, in 2017, *"Star Trek: Discovery"* debuted. Currently CBS All Access is available only in the United States and Canada (limited) and on Roku and Chromecast.

- **CuriosityStream** (curiositystream.com). $2.99 per month. They offer more than fifteen hundred science, history, tech, and nature documentaries. Available on multiple devices.

- **Crunchyroll** (crunchyroll.com). $6.95 per month. Devoted primarily to anime and live-action Asian TV. It offers 1,000 shows, more than 30,000 streaming episodes, and some of the best Korean and Chinese films.

- **Tribeca Shortlist** (tribecashortlist.com). $4.99 per month. A platform that features some very popular films, such as *"Capote"*, *"Amores Perros"*, *"La Cage Aux Folles"*, and *"Inherit the Wind"*.

- **Sundance Now** (sundancenow.com). $4.99 per month. As the name suggests, they offer independent and influential dramas, comedies, documentaries, and miniseries, many from past Sundance Festivals.

Conclusion

Subscribing to too many platforms can be expensive. Check periodically and calculate how many films you've seen on each platform during the last quarter. The two that will probably give you your money's worth are Netflix and Amazon Prime. If you're subscribing to a platform just to see one specific film or film series, you'll probably be able to fit this in during the free-trial period. You can then cancel the subscription after you finish watching the film or series. To avoid cancellations, the platforms are under pressure to provide their subscribers with a continuous flow of new films. It's probably the reason why only the most financially strong companies will survive.

Fanny Ward & Sessue Hayakawa
Cecil B Demille's "The Cheat"
December 13th 1915

8
Advertising-Supported Video on Demand (AVOD) Platforms

"Most filmmakers can't afford to try something that doesn't work."
—Francis Ford Coppola

Advertising execs universally agree that the most compelling way to market a product is to say that it's free.

The same applies to streaming films. By adding some advertising before the film begins, these AVOD platforms can offer free movies.

Here are five caveats about the platforms listed in this chapter.

1. Currently they cannot transmit films in 4K or Ultra High Definition. Instead, these services provide regular HD video, similar to what you get from the cable companies.

2. The latest films and TV shows will probably not be available.

3. In some cases it will not be easy to fast-forward through the ads.

4. If advertising drops, some of the platforms may go out of business.

5. To stream these channels, you'll need a smartphone, tablet, smart TV, PlayStation 3 or 4, or current Xbox.

Hulu terminated its free advertising-supported platform, which was a big loss. Hulu is now a subscription only service (See chapter 5). However, there are still a few good players left.

- **Facebook Watch** (facebook.com/watch). In announcing this spinoff, Facebook will have a lineup that will appeal to its vast audience: shows obtained from TV channels, live sports, reality TV, and original productions. The site will also include personalized recommendations from viewers. With over 500 million daily viewers watching videos on Facebook, it's not surprising that they have decided to compete with Netflix and Amazon.

- **Crackle** (sonycrackle.com). It's a Sony, ad-supported service. It has a library of older TV shows and popular classic movies. It's starting to invest in original programming.

- **Watch Documentaries** (watchdocumentaries.com). They have more than 9,000 quality documentaries in their library. Docs can be seen on any Android device. Currently they are not available on Apple devices.

- **Pluto TV** (pluto.tv). They offer video content curated from the web as well as past hit films and classics.

- **Roku Channel** (roku.com). Roku will be using part of the money from its $100 million initial public offering to set up this ad-supported channel. Initially, they will draw films from MGM, Sony, Warner, and Lionsgate.

- **Tubi TV** (tubitv.com). Its more than 7,000 titles include selections from the libraries of Lionsgate, MGM, Paramount, and Starz. A valuable feature is that Tubi TV will allow you to pause the film and then resume watching it later on.

- **Vudu** (vudu.com). It draws its full-length feature films from all the major movie studios as well as from independent distributors. Hopefully, they will soon produce and offer original movies.

- **XUMO** (xumo.tv). XUMO focuses on content from the premium channels like the Onion, TMZ, GQ, NBC News, and the PGA. It is hoped that they will soon offer movies.

- **SnagFilms** (snagfilms.com). Their specialty is the indie film, or what they call the hidden movie treasures. They now have 5,000 films in their library.

- **Popcornnflix** (popcornflix.com). This site offers movies in many genres including animation, horror, comedy, suspense, action, and drama.

Conclusion

With its huge base, Apple Watch should lead the AVOD pack. However, with an infusion of capital from the public offering of stock, the Roku Channel also has a promising future.

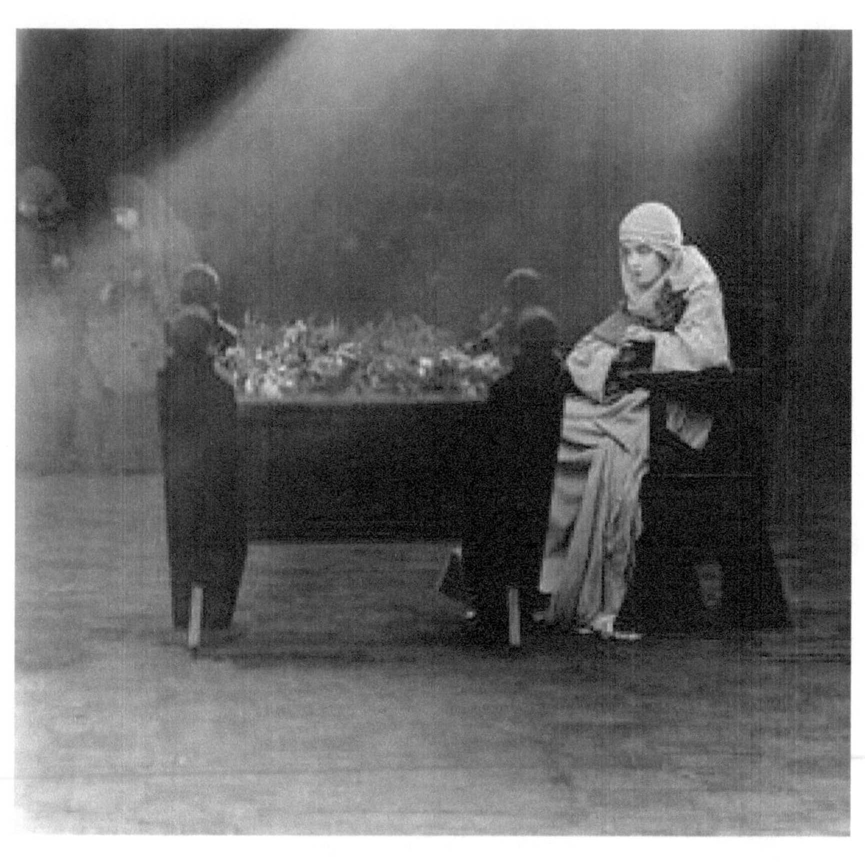

Mae Marsh "Intolerance"
September 5th 1916

9
Free Films with No Advertising

"I don't guess what a million people will like. It's hard for me to know what I'd like."

—John Huston

In the previous chapter on Advertising-Supported platforms (AVOD), we listed a few of the majors. In all of those cases, you'll have to endure a stretch of advertising before the film appears.

The following services offer free films with no advertising because most operate as non-profits and receive grants and donations. A few are connected and funded by their local libraries and educational institutions.

Unfortunately, many of these services offering free movies can disappear, some quite suddenly. A good way of keeping track of what is out there currently is by viewing the website, bestfreestreaming.com.

Here are a few platforms to consider.

- **Kanopy** (kanopy.com). To use this service, you'll need a membership at a participating library, university, or other learning institution. Their 26,000+ films are drawn from such sources as the Criterion Collection, the Great Courses, New Day Films, and PBS. It's a very cerebral platform.

- **Vudu** (vudu.com). Vudu is generally considered an ad-supported platform (See Chapter 7). However, if you go to the top of its Home page and click "Movies On Us," you'll see a rundown of free movies with no advertising. This lineup is not as extensive as its lineup on its ad-supported program, but you never know what you'll find.

- **CMoviesHD** (cmovieshd.is). They sort their films by genre and include a story line for each film.

- **Hoopla** (hoopladigital.com). Hoopla operates like Kanopy in that you can watch films for free if your local public library or educational institution is on board. Don't expect too many current films but their lineup is big enough to please most viewers. They obtain movies by securing rights from major Hollywood studios and distributors.

- **Internet Archive** (archive.org). Internet Archive is a non-profit library service offering viewers access to millions of books. However, they also offer 3,000+ films, mostly old classics.

- **YouTube** (youtube.com). In addition to the usual clips and films, YouTube also offers free movies in the public domain. They've had some bad publicity regarding the inclusion of illegally-obtained movies. However, they are making strides in spotting these movies.

- **Classic Cinema** (classiccinema.org). Classic Cinema offers free movies ranging from old cult classics to new independent films. They also feature short films, documentaries, animated films, stand-up comedy, and TV shows. They offer such films as *"How Green Was My Valley"*, *"Stagecoach"*, *"Rebecca"*, and *"City Lights"*.

- **Viewster** (viewster.com). Viewster focuses more on international films. They have abundant content from cult to classic, Japanese anime, British, Korean, and Swedish dramas.

Conclusion
The best deals are the platforms being offered by your local library or educational institution. The three most popular are Kanopy, Hoopla, and Internet Archive. Check out Kanopy if you're partial to old classics as they offer the great films in the Criterion Collection.

Warner Oland & Irene Castle "Patria"
January 14th 1917

10
Amazon Channels: A New Service

"The secret of film is that it's an illusion."
—George Lucas

This new service from Amazon allows subscribers the convenience to pick and choose from more than 100 streaming channels. You'll still pay the normal rate for each channel you choose, but Amazon Channels has the following advantages:

- One-stop billing. No need to leave your credit card information with multiple channels. You are essentially subscribing to a third-party streaming service through your Amazon account.

- Convenience. Each channel has different procedures required to access their site. Now you can have Amazon hook you up with any site on their list without the hassle.

- There is no additional cost other than the cost of being an Amazon Prime subscriber and the cost of each channel accessed.

- Having a free trial subscription available with each channel is ideal if you want to watch just one film or film series and that's all. One disadvantage with this program, however is that the free trial subscription is for only seven days rather than the usual thirty days.

- There are no setup or cancellation fees, nor is there any minimum.

- After you've started an Amazon Channel subscription, you can watch the movies on all your compatible Prime Video devices.

- Most third-party channels will give you the option to watch programming on supported devices at the same time as the TV broadcast.

- Viewers can interact with Amazon Channels using Alexa.

- You can watch content just about anywhere, including on Android devices, iPhones, tablets, and smart TVs.

- You only have to remember one username and password.

To start an Amazon Channel subscription, you'll have to be an Amazon Prime member. Amazon will recognize any of the following types of memberships.

- Amazon Prime

- Thirty-day Amazon Prime free trial

- Amazon Prime Student membership

- Prime Student free trial

- Amazon Prime free preview

- Amazon Prime Fresh

- Thirty-Day Amazon Prime Fresh free trial

- Amazon Household Shared Prime Benefits

Currently, Amazon Channels does not have an agreement with Netflix or Hulu. This could change by the time this guide is published.

Amazon Channels can connect you with more than 100 streaming sites. Some of the better ones are: HBO, Showtime, Cinemax, Starz, MUBI, Sundance Now, Sports Illustrated, Comic Con HQ, History Vault, Comedy Central Stand-Up, PBS Masterpiece, IndiePix Unlimited, DocComTV, Smithsonian Earth, Reelz, Daily Burn, PBS Kids, Shudder, and Cheddar.

Competition? You bet. Roku and Apple will shortly have similar services to compete with Amazon Channels.

How to Navigate Amazon Channels.

1. You must first subscribe to the channel of your choice. For more information, search "what are prime video channel subscriptions?"

2. Open Prime Video and look for "Your Channels." Select one of your channels to browse available films or series.

3. When you find something you want to watch, select "Watch Now," just like you would for any other Prime Video title.

Conclusion
If you're already a subscriber to Amazon Prime or other Amazon-related programs, then you have nothing to lose by subscribing to Amazon Channels. You'll thus enjoy all the benefits previously listed without incurring additional cost. If you are not an Amazon Prime subscriber, this program will only make sense if the benefits listed above are worth the cost of becoming an Amazon Prime subscriber.

Charlie Chaplan's "The Immigrant"
June 17th 1917

11
Public Domain Films

"A wide screen just makes a bad film twice as bad."
—Samuel Goldwyn

Public domain films can be shown freely because no person, government, or organization has any proprietary rights to these films. They are not owned or controlled by any of these entities. These films are available to anyone, free of charge. Most of these films can be seen on the built-in browser in your TV.

There are three major reasons why films end up in the public domain.

- They did not renew or register their copyrights by the deadline date.

- Their copyright is flawed.

- They were made by US government employees as part of their official duties.

Unfortunately, there is no official list of films in the public domain. It's not easy for the average person to find out about these films or how to see them. The surest and most reliable way is to access these films from one of the platforms offering public domain films.

Here's the methodology.

1. Select the platform that interests you.

2. Sign up for a free membership (if required).

3. Scroll the category that interests you.

4. Click the film you want to watch.

5. A new page will appear with a rectangle enclosing an arrow.

6. Click the arrow and watch the film.

There are many platforms with websites that offer free movies, most of them in the public domain. Watch out! Many of them are operating illegally, offering pirated films. The service Public Domain Flicks (publicdomainflicks.com) offers some tips to help you identify legal websites.

1. A legal website will tell you its sources. Look for the "About Us" section to find the source information.

2. Unless it's a nonprofit, a legal website will include advertising.

3. A legal website will probably not offer the latest films.

4. A legal website often has a mobile app.

5. A legal website will have a "Contact" section.

Here are the major public domain platforms and a few of their most prominent films.

- **Internet Archive** (archive.org). *"The Fast and the Furious"* (1955), *"Utopia"* (1951), *"House on the Haunted Hill"* (1959), *"Jungle Book"* (1942), *"Dressed to Kill"* (1946), *"My Man Godfrey"* (1936), *"The Stranger"* (1946), *"The Phantom of the Opera"* (1925), *"As You Like It"* (1936), *"Meet John Doe"* (1941), *"The Little Princess"* (1939), *"Royal Wedding"* (1951).

- **Public Domain Flix** (publicdomainflix.com). *"The Strange Love of Martha Ivers"* (1946), *"Beau*

Brummel" (1924), "Street Scene" (1931), "The Phantom of the Opera" (1925), "The Nazis Strike" (1943), "Indestructible Man" (1956).

- **Public Domain Movies** (publicdomainmovies.net). "Charlie Chaplin Festival" (1917), "His Girl Friday" (1940), "Plan 9 from Outer Space" (1959), "Abraham Lincoln" (1930), "Gulliver's Travels" (1939), "Suddenly" (1954), "My Man Godfrey" (1936), "The Stranger" (1946), "Battleship Potemkin" (1925), "Popeye for President" (1956).

- **The Video Cellar** (thevideocellar.com). "Terror by Night" (1946), "The Invisible Ghost" (1941), "British Intelligence" (1940), "The Sin of Nora Moran" (1933).

- **Uncle Earl's Classic Television** (solie.org/classicTV). "The Mark of Zorro" (1920), "The Emperor Jones" (1933), "The Call of the Wild" (1935), "The Son of Monte Cristo" (1940), "Jungle Man" (1941), "A Yank in Libya" (1942), "And Then There Were None" (1944).

- **Classic Movies EZ** (classicmoviesez.com). "A Star Is Born" (1937), "Born to Win" (1971), "C-Man" (1949), "Comedy of Terror" (1963), "Fit for a King" (1937), "Friday the Thirteenth" (1933), "Destination Space" (1959).

- **Big Five Glories** (bigfiveglories.com). "The Birth of a Nation" (1915), "Charlie Chan's Secret" (1936), "The Ghost Train" (1941), "Reefer Madness" (1938), "The Kid" (1921), "Heel's House" (1932).

- **Open Culture Films** (openculture.com). "Beat the Devil" (1954), "Borderline" (1950), "Cause for Alarm!" (1951), "Five Minutes to Live" (1961), "Impact" (1940), "Johnny O'Clock" (1947), "The Hitch-Hiker" (1953),

"The Strange Love of Martha Ivers" (1946), *"The Stranger"* (1946).

Conclusion

As you'll note, you'll find few recent films in the public domain. Most were released prior to 1960 and some may even go back to the days before sound. But they are free, so what the heck!

12
Streaming Special Interest Films by Category

> *"Man is a genius when he is dreaming."*
> —Akira Kurosawa

For almost every special interest there is a platform streaming such films. This chapter lists some of these special interest platforms by category. The films listed are primarily made by up-and-coming independent filmmakers who depend on these platforms to get their films launched. It's unlikely that you'll find the more popular, well-known films in each category. For these you'll have to search the major platforms like Netflix and Amazon.

I've listed the popular films available in each category. This will give you an idea of the sort of content they offer.

Documentaries

These are fact-based (nonfiction) films that generally do not employ professional actors except as narrators. They are mainly produced for instruction, educating viewers, and for recording historical events.

- **Top Documentary Films** (topdocumentaryfilms.com). Free. Included are reviews from trusted sources, and comments and opinions from viewers. The documentaries are classified in categories making it easy to find the films that interest you. Popular films: *"Kim Jong Un: The Unauthorized Biography"*, *"Sea the Truth: The Environment"*, *"Richard Feynman: Fun to Imagine"*, *"The Greatest Animal Migration"*, *"Israel's Secret Weapon"*.

- **Documentary Heaven** (documentaryheaven.com). Free. An unusual platform in that none of the content is hosted on the site. The movies are taken from other sites, such as Vimeo and YouTube. Popular films: *"Jefferson"*, *"The Trap: Human Trafficking"*, *"The Kim Dynasty"*.

- **Documentary Storm** (documentarystorm.com). Free. The focus is on nature, animals, natural phenomenon, the ocean, plants, and prehistoric life. Popular films: *"Orca Rescue"*, *"Twisted"*, *"The Last of the Rhinos"*, *"Insecta: Science That Stings"*, *"The Living Forest"*, *"Cry of the Wild"*.

- **Documentary Tube** (documentarytube.com). Free. This platform offers a large number of educational and historical films. Popular films: *"Japan: The History of Japan's Ancient and Modern Empire"*, *"Carthage: The Roman Holocaust"*, *"Farmlands: The Plight of South African Farmers"*, *"Benedict Arnold, Elon Musk: How I Became the Iron Man"*.

- **Films for Action** (filmsforaction.org). Free. Offering perhaps the largest online learning library for social change. Popular films: *"1980s Movies That Shaped Our Humanity"*, *"A Lighthouse for Gaza"*, *"Islamophobia"*, *"The Economics of Happiness"*.

- **Free Documentaries** (freedocumentaries.org). Free. This organization has researchers who scour the web for thought-provoking (sometimes controversial), educational documentaries. Popular films: *"Stealing Africa"*, *"The Trials of Henry Kissinger"*, *"The Panama Deception"*, *"The U.S. vs. John Lennon"*.

- **DocumentaryWIRE** (documentarywire.com). Free. One of the few free platforms offering some of the more current documentaries. Popular films: *"Sicko"*, *"Fahrenheit 9/11"*, *"Supersize Me, Off the Grid"*.

- **Documentary 24** (documentary24.com). Free. Offers a wide range of documentary topics: war, conspiracy, science, lifestyle, history, biography, business, culture, and nature. Popular films: *"Wildlife–Serengeti"*, *"Greece Bankruptcy"*, *"The Islamic State"*, *"The History of Writing"*.

- **The Documentary Network** (documentary.net). Free. Offers a wide range of topics that you can search by category. Popular films: *"The Collapse of Venezuela Explained"*, *"The Happiest People on Earth—North Koreans"*, *"Rebranding White Nationalism: Inside Richard Spencer's Alt-Right"*.

- **Documentary Addict** (documentaryaddict.com). Free. A wide-ranging platform offering 5,400 documentaries in twenty-six categories. Popular films: *"Food Inc."*, *"Why Beauty Matters"*, *"Going Clear: Scientology and the Prison of Belief"*, *"Enron—The Smartest Guys in the Room."*

Classic Films

These are films that transcend trends and hold up favorably over the passage of time. In effect, classic films have become part of American culture. In addition to the list below, many classic films are offered by public domain platforms (See chapter 10).

- **FilmStruck** (filmstruck.com). $6.99 per month (basic plan), $10.99 per month or $99 annually (basic plan + the Criterion Collection). With access to the Criterion Collection and TCM, this is the ultimate streaming service for fans of classic films. Popular films: *"Edward, My Son"*, *"Rio Bravo"*, *"PT 109"*, *"Grey Gardens"*.

- **Kanopy** (kanopy.com). Free if you join a participating library or educational institution. With more than 30,000 films, this is a treasure trove of international classics. Popular films: *"Charade"*, *"Metropolis"*, *"Bicycle Thief"*, *"Girlhood"*, *"Loving Vincent"*.

Film Noir

The literal translation for film noir is "black film" or "dark film." They are primarily crime-story films released in the 40s and 50s that feature hardboiled characters and fatalistic endings. Many of the popular film noir films were adaptations of novels by Raymond Chandler, James Cain, and Dashiell Hammett. The more popular film noir films can be seen on Netflix, HBO, and Hulu. The following two platforms offer many lesser-known selections.

- **Open Culture Films** (openculture.com). Free. Popular films: *"D.O.A."*, *"He Walked by Night"*, *"Johnny O'Clock"*, *"The Great St. Louis Bank Robbery"*, *"The Red House"*, *"Woman on the Run"*.

- **Moviewatcher** (moviewatcher.is). Free. Popular films: *"Body and Soul"*, *"Sunset Boulevard"*, *"He Ran All the Way"*, *"Sweet Smell of Success"*, *"A Kiss Before Dying"*, *"Blue Dahlia"*, *"Double Indemnity"*, *"Strangers on a Train"*.

Horror

Horror films do their job if they scare you, make you cringe, make you feel creepy, or sometimes make you laugh when they are over-the-top campy.

- **FrightPix** (frightpix.com). Free. As a division of Screen Media Ventures, FrightPix offers a wide range of high-quality horror films. Popular films: *"A Tale of Two Sisters"*, *"The Attic"*, *"Alice in Murderland"*, *"Home Sweet Home"*, *"Kinky Killers"*, *"Dark Night of the Scarecrow"*, *"Hayride"*, *"Night of the Living Dead"*.

- **Shudder Films** (shudder.com). $4.99 per month or $47.88 annually. In addition to their extensive library of horror films, they add new films on a weekly basis. Popular films: *"Alyce Kills"*, *"Truth or Die"*, *"Crawl"*, *"The Woman"*, *"Beast from the Haunted Cave"*, *"Haunting Helena"*.

- **Screambox Films** (screambox.com). $4.99 per month or $35.88 annually. The focus is on monster films, the supernatural, killers, and psychological films. Popular films: *"Brain Dead"*, *"Werewolf Fever"*, *"Alien Psychosis"*, *"Little Shop of Horrors"*.

Sports

Most of these platforms feature live or recorded sporting events. Sports-themed features (usually biographical) can be seen on the major platforms like Netflix, Amazon, and iTunes.

- **ESPN+** (watch.espnplus.com). $4.99 per month. This is a new streaming service from ESPN. When in season, you'll be able to see live sports coverage of MLB, MLS, and NHL. Also when in season, PGA golf, top-ranked boxing, and Grand Slam tennis. The platform provides three categories: Upcoming, Live Now, and Replay. In their first year they got over one million subscribers.

- **Stream2watch** (stream2watch.me). Free. This site offers live streaming of major sporting events, and a list of the times when these events start.

- **MLBTV** (mlb.tv) $24.99 per season, including spring
  training games. Watch current major league games
  and full game archives of previous seasons. Each
  game is available in HD with pause and rewind
  functionality. Blackout and other restrictions may
  apply.

  Several platforms are excellent for watching a wide
  variety of international and US sporting events. Many
  offer these events in several different languages.
  They are free and provide easy links to each event.
  Try these: Streaming Sports (streamingsports.me),
  SportLemon (sportlemon.net), and First Row Sports
  (firstsrowsports.tv).

Music

All the major platforms offer narrative and documentary films
with musical themes. The following platforms offer major
concerts and musical performances.

- **YouTube Music Premium**
  (youtube.com/musicpremium). $9.99 per month. It's a
  hefty cost to those accustomed to listening for free on
  the basic YouTube channel. But this new service is a
  completely reimagined site offering original albums,
  concerts, and more.

- **Stingray Qello** (qello.com). $7.99 per month. A
  streaming service offering full-length concerts and
  documentaries on demand.

British Films

Many great historical, detective, mysteries, soaps, and socially relevant films come from Britain, Ireland, and Australia. The following are three good platforms featuring such films.

- **BBC America** (bbcamerica.com). Free. This is a commercially supported platform that accepts advertising. Popular films: *"Doctor Who", "Killing Eve", "Dietland", "BBC Earth Specials".*

- **Acorn TV** (support.acorn.tv). $5 a month or $50 a year. Popular films: *"A Place to Call Home", "Foyle's War", "Vera", "Doc Martin", "Agatha Christie's Marple".*

- **BritBox** (britbox.com). $6.99 per month. They classify their films in four categories: Drama (*"Churchill's Darkest Hour", "Poldark"*); Mystery (*"Vera, Maigret"*); Comedy (*"Marley's Ghost", "Are You Being Served?"*); and Doc/Lifestyle (*"Britain's Secret Treasures", "Trooping the Colours"*).

Bollywood Films

India has become a very important movie-making country.

- **Viewlorium** (viewlorium.com). Free. Popular films: *"Seducing Maarya", "Kasme Vaade", "Alwan", "Tere Naam", "Astitva".*

Asian Films

Primarily from Korea, Taiwan, and Japan.

- **Viki** (viki.com). $8.33 per month or $99.99 annually. Popular films: *"The Legend of the Blue Sea"*, *"Siege in Fog"*, *"Radio Romance"*, *"Here to Heart"*, *"While You Were Sleeping"*.

- **AsianCrush** (asiancrush.com). Free. Popular films: *"Goku"*, *"Lily C.A.T."*, *"The Twelve Kingdoms"*, *"Samaritan Girl"*.

- **Crunchyroll** (crunchyroll.com). $6.99 per month, $19.95 for 3 months, or $59.95 annually. Included in their lineup of 30,000 episodes are some of the best Korean and Chinese films.

Kids' Films

Many films for young audiences are available on most platforms. This one stands out.

- **Kanopy Kids** (kanopy.com/kids). Free if you belong to a participating library or educational institution. They offer a fantastic selection in different categories: Story Time Classics (*"I Want My Hat Back"*, *"Don't Let the Pigeon Stay Up Late"*, *"Curious George Rides a Bike"*); Movies for Younger Kids (*"Charlotte's Web"*, *"Bon Voyage, Charlie Brown"*, *"Ernest & Celestine"*); Movies for Older Kids (*"A Cat in Paris"*, *"Albion: The Enchanted Stallion"*); Learning about Science, Math, and Nature (*"Nature Cat"*, *"Ready Jet Go"*, *"Splash and Bubbles"*); Literary Classics (*"Cinderella"*, *"Where the Wild Things Are"*).

- **Popcornflix** (popcornflix.site). Free. They offer a huge selection of films geared for kids. Last time I looked, they offered such films as "Jack on the Beanstalk," "Mee-She," and "School of Life."

Conclusion

Many of the platforms listed above are free. However, most of the films they offer will not be well-known, and are primarily produced by independent filmmakers and nonprofit organizations. Who knows, you may discover a few films that are true gems.

John Ford "Straight Shooter"
August 27th 1917

13
Helpful Hints

"Movies take you right up to the edge but keep you safe."
—John Updike

1. Buying last year's TV model will reduce the cost. In most cases, features do not change materially from one year to the next. Also, you'll often save if you buy on Black Friday (the day after Thanksgiving) and the day after Christmas.

2. For best quality, disable other internet connections while streaming. Your picture will look best if the streaming of the film is the only service connected to the internet.

3. An Ethernet connector will often produce better results than a wireless connector.

4. After buying a new TV, consider hiring a professional or a local technician (geek) to calibrate and fine-tune it.

5. Make sure you get the largest size TV you can afford and one that's appropriate for the room. One measurement is to sit at least as far back as the TV screen size. So if you have a sixty-five-inch TV, make sure that you can sit at least five and a half feet from the TV.

6. HDRs, which deliver a brighter picture, are not all the same. A few fail to reach promised results. To be sure, check the HDR scores published by Consumer Reports.

7. To get the full rundown of the massive Netflix library, check the following websites: instantwatcher.com

and whats-on-netflix.com. Also check chapter 13 for additional newsletters that will be helpful.

8.   Do not think that the picture quality you see on the TV in the showroom will be the same when you watch the same TV at home. The TVs in the showroom are often enhanced and charged up to brighten the picture to much higher levels.

9.   Signing up for too many subscription (SVOD) platforms can be expensive. Many people sign up to watch a particular film that is only available on that platform. This can be a good deal as most platforms offer a free period before the charge kicks in. It then makes sense to cancel the subscription after watching the movie or the series, if you do not intend to view anything else on the platform.

10.   Everyone, both frequent and infrequent movie watchers, should sign up with the transactional video on demand (TVOD) platforms because they charge only when you click to watch a movie. For this same reason, you should subscribe to the platforms offering free movies. (See chapters 5, 8, and 10.)

11.   A TV with a built-in media streamer (like Android, Roku, or Apple) will make accessing content much easier. (See chapter 3.)

12.   Most LCD TVs have limited viewing angles. If this bothers you, consider buying an OLED TV. It provides good viewing from many different angles. If you often have several people watching the same show, avoid a TV with a curved screen, which exaggerates the angles when viewing from the side.

13.   If you are already an Amazon shopping customer, you're entitled to have the Amazon Prime streaming

service for no extra cost. If you are not an Amazon shopper, then opt for Amazon Instant Video and pay only for the films you want to watch.

14. If you are unhappy with Netflix's standard yellow subtitles, you can select eight different colors as well as the background color that appears behind the text. These options can be selected by going to the "Account" page on the Netflix website and then clicking "Subtitle preferences."

15. Students should check to see if the streaming platforms they want offer a student discount.

16. Make sure the TV you buy has the required number and type of connections to hook up equipment, such as an external streaming media player (if it doesn't have one built in), game console, external hard drive, and a sound bar. (see Chapter 1)

17. If you're buying a TV set larger than forty inches, select one with 4K UHD. For a TV smaller than forty inches, HD should be adequate.

18. To improve your TV picture when streaming a film, reduce the number of obstacles between your router and the TV.

19. Keep track of the number of films you've watched on each subscription platform. At the end of the quarter, calculate whether the cost justified the number of films watched. If not, unsubscribe and save the money.

20. The Apple Media Streamer will give you both Amazon Instant Video and iTunes, the two most popular transactional (pay-per-film) platforms.

21. Picture stuttering and freezing of the picture is probably related to bandwidth. This can usually be fixed by requesting a faster pipe from your internet service provider.

22. As cable companies like HBO and Showtime start offering their own streaming services, you may want to calculate whether it makes more sense to cancel your cable subscription and replace it with the streaming subscription. The added advantage of the streaming subscription is that you can replay old shows you may have missed or want to watch again.

23. You will not regret getting a universal remote control. My recommendation is the Logitech Harmony Ultimate One (logitech.com).

24. If you are not pleased with the sound from your TV, the solution is to add a sound bar or sound base. (See chapter 2)

25. If your TV comes with a built-in media streamer like Apple, Amazon, Roku, or Chromecast, it may still lack platforms you would like to have. The solution is to purchase an external media streamer. (See chapter 3)

26. Purchase a dual-band router rather than a single-band router. One connects to the 2.4GHz band and the other connects to the 5 GHz band. The 5 GHz band is less crowded and ideal for video streaming.

27. Don't throw out your DVD and Blu-ray discs. As Dan Sullivan at *CNET* writes, "Giving up on discs means giving up control. You're giving up the ability to absolutely, positively know that the movie or TV show you own is available to watch at the highest

possible quality, without some terms of service down the road possibly taking it away."[18]

28. Before buying an extended warranty, check with your credit card company. They may offer protection at no cost.

29. Most homes will only need 10 Mbps although the Federal Communications Commission recently updated its definition of broadband to a minimum of 25 Mpbs. You will, however, need a relatively fast connection, between 15 Mpbs to 25 Mpbs, to stream 4K content.

30. If you're buying a media streamer like the ones described in chapter 3, you might consider adding an external hard drive. You can then store those classic films you want to watch again and again.

Conclusion

Do you have any tips we should add? If so, please email them to us at info@accessingfilms.com, and we'll include them in our next edition.

---

[18] "How Trapped Are Your Digital Movies and TV Shows?" Danny Sullivan, CNET, January 31, 2013, www.cnet.com/news/how-trapped-are-your-digital-movies-and-tv-shows/.

Theda Bara "Cleopatra"
October 14th 1917

14
Recommended Film Series

"It's all just one film to me. Just different chapters."
—Robert Altman

Each recommended film series listed below is available through most of 2018 and should continue to be available through 2019. However, each platform has an individual agreement with the filmmaker, studio, or distributor. When the agreement expires, and if it's not renewed, the film is pulled from the platform. Also, a platform may pull a film if it's not active. We do not always receive advance notice nor do we have control over these cancellations. Our apologies if that's the case with any of the films listed here.

To avoid such disappointments, check the platform's website. Click 'Search' to see if the film is still being offered. The website should also indicate if additional series are planned.

Films that are not spoken in English will have subtitles. Most English-speaking films offer closed-captioning as well.

I have not listed well-known series, such as *"The Crown"*, *"Game of Thrones"*, or *"Orange Is the New Black"*. The series listed below are probably not that well known, but they are listed because they are well-worth viewing.

Many platforms are preparing additional seasons. To keep informed, subscribe (it's free) to each platform's newsletter.

"A French Village"
MHz Choice (watch.mhzchoice.com)
French and German
7 seasons (72 episodes). Each episode is between 42 and
55 minutes.

In June 1940, German military forces occupy the fictional
French village of Villeneuve. They quickly take control of all
aspects of the village's life and businesses. All political
dissent and resistance are brutally suppressed. German
officers put pressure on the locals to engage in roundups
and to meet strict Jewish deportation quotas. Many villagers
collaborate with the Germans. After liberation, the
collaborators are vilified and some are executed.

"The Bridge"
Amazon Prime and Amazon Instant Video (amazon.com)
Swedish and Danish
2 seasons (20 episodes). Each episode is 60 minutes.

A corpse, cut in half at the waistline, is found on the bridge
connecting Sweden and Denmark. Danish inspector Martin
Rohde and Swedish inspector, Saga Noren, must share
jurisdiction and work together to find the killer. There are
many twists and turns as the killers are obsessed with
violations to the environment and correcting social injustices.
Complicating the investigations are the personal lives of
Saga and Martin.

"Ozark"
Netflix (netflix.com)
English
1 season (9 episodes). Each episode is 60 minutes

A financial planner involved in money-laundering schemes
for a drug cartel, is forced to move with his family to the
Ozarks after one of his schemes goes bad. Hoping to make

amends, he sets out to launch a money-laundering scheme in a small town in the Ozarks. He gets involved with local criminals and his situation becomes even more dangerous.

"Safe Harbour"
Hulu (hulu.com)
English
1 season (4 episodes). Each episode is between 54 and 61 minutes

Five Australians are on a yacht heading for Indonesia when they spot a fishing boat filled with desperate asylum seekers. They begin towing the boat to safety but the boat sinks killing seven of the refugees. Five years later, in this gripping thriller, the Australians are still grappling with everything that happened that night.

"Fauda"
Netflix (netflix.com)
Hebrew and Arabic
2 seasons (12 episodes). Each episode is 45 minutes

Filmed primarily in the occupied West Bank, the plot revolves around the conflicts between Israeli Special Forces and Hamas. There are brutal attacks by both sides. As expected, these events cause family conflicts and pain to both Palestinian and Israeli families. Taut and suspenseful.

"The Marvelous Mrs. Maisel"
Amazon Prime (amazon.com/prime)
English
1 season (8 episodes). Each episode is between 46 and 60 minutes

A hilarious comedy about a young Jewish housewife (Mrs. Maisel) in 1958 New York who discovers that she has a talent for stand-up comedy. Her success breaks up her marriage and creates problems with her old-fashioned family. The star is the vivacious, Emmy-winner, Rachel Brosnahan.

"The Night Of"
HBO NOW (hbonow.com) and HBO GO (hbogo.com)
English
1 season (8 episodes). Each episode is between 56 and 96 minutes.

A riveting crime drama of a naive Pakistani-American student (a terrific performance by Riz Ahmed) living in Queens. One night he takes his father's cab to a party and picks up a young woman who seduces him. When he wakes up the next morning he finds her dead, savagely stabbed. He's caught, indicted, and spends a stretch at Rikers Island. Did he kill the woman or was he too drunk to really know? A brilliant John Turturro is his lawyer who is trying to reverse what he considers an injustice.

"Picnic at Hanging Rock"
Amazon Prime and Amazon Instant Video (Amazon.com)
English
1 season (8 episodes). Each episode is 60 minutes

This Australian drama is an adaptation of Joan Lindsay's 1967 novel. It's about a group of schoolgirls who disappear while on an outing to Hanging Rock in 1900. The controversial parts of the story are a dangerous romance between a schoolgirl and her teacher and same-sex kisses between two other girls.

"A Place to Call Home"
Acorn TV (acorn.tv)
English

6 seasons (62 episodes). Each episode is between 42 and 45 minutes.

The series is set in New South Wales, Australia shortly after the end of World War II. Sarah Adams returns home after living abroad for twenty years. She intends to start a new life but instead ends up with multiple issues and heartache.

"Big Little Lies"
HBO NOW (hbonow.com) and HBO GO (hbogo.com)
English
1 season (7 episodes). Each episode is between 52 and 58 minutes.

Created and written by David E. Kelley, the series stars Nicole Kidman, Reese Witherspoon, and Shailene Woodley. They play three emotionally troubled women in Monterey, California and how they become embroiled in a murder investigation.

"Spiral"
MHz Choice (watch.mhzchoice.com)
French
6 seasons (64 episodes). Each episode is 52 minutes.

The series depicts the lives and the activities of French police officers, lawyers, and judges at the Palais de Justice.

"Babylon Berlin"
Netflix (netflix.com)
German
2 seasons (16 episodes). Each episode is 45 minutes.

This crime drama takes place in 1929, during the Weimar Republic. It deals with the crimes being investigated by police inspector Gereon Rath and the aggressive police inspector, Charlotte Ritter. The series captures the coming dangers of pre-Hitler Germany.

"Collateral"
Netflix (netflix.com)
English
1 season (4 episodes). Each episode is 60 minutes.

This police drama, written and created by David Hare, is about a detective (Carey Mulligan) assigned to investigate the murder of a pizza delivery driver, killed in a London suburb.

"Spring Tide"
MHz Choice (watch.mhzchoice.com)
Swedish
1 season (10 episodes). Each episode is 43 minutes.

Olivia Ronning, a trainee at the Swedish Police Academy, is assigned to investigate the unsolved twenty-five-year-old sadistic murder of a pregnant woman. When she learns that her late father worked on the original case, she becomes obsessed with finding the murderer.

"Narcos"
Netflix (netflix.com)
Spanish
3 seasons (30 episodes). Each episode is between 43 and 60 minutes.

Filmed in Colombia, the first two seasons are about the drug lord, Pablo Escobar, who became a billionaire by processing and selling cocaine. Season three continues the story after Escobar is killed with the DEA's pursuit of the Cali Cartel.

Conclusion
Great films are now being streamed. In order to add more paying subscribers, the platforms must keep coming up with a continuous flow of good content. More like the above are sure to come.

**Alice Mann, Roscoe 'Fatty' Arbuckle & Buster Keaton,
"Coney Island"
October 29th 1917**

15
Subscriptions and Books

> *"The more opinions you have, the less you see."*
> —Wim Wenders

The landscape for streaming films has become so vast that we're now seeing a proliferation of informative newsletters and books on this subject.

This may be too much for the average film buff to digest. However, some of the newsletters that have recently popped up can be very helpful in guiding the viewer to what's out there. And, here's the good part: all the newsletters listed in this chapter are free.

Newsletters

- *Watching* (NYTimes.com/watching). Published by *The New York Times*, this newsletter covers the gamut of general news and recommending films on both cable stations and the internet platforms.

- *Inside Streaming* (insidestreaming.com/streaming). This is primarily a breaking news type of newsletter. However, it also includes a rundown of what's coming on the major platforms.

- *Inside* (inside.com/streaming). News, updates, reviews, and analysis of industry and consumer trends in the world of streaming.

- *The Guardian* (theguardian.com/uk/film). A rundown of the most popular British films being streamed. It also includes essays and reviews.

- *Decider* (decider.com). A combination of news and a listing of the latest films being streamed.

- *StreamDaily* (streamdaily.tv/subscribe/newsletter). Covers the business side of online-video entertainment.

- *Couragez* (couragez.com). Gives you a day-by-day lineup of films worth streaming. Major focus on foreign-language films.

- *IndieWire* (indiewire.com). Covers the wider scope of news about upcoming independent films. Each issue includes one or two stories about what's happening with digital film streaming.

- *New Day Films* (newday.com/content/about-streaming). *New Day Films* is a unique filmmaker-run distribution company. Through its newsletter, it informs educators, community groups, government agencies, and public libraries about many of the films available for streaming, some of them award winners.

Most streaming platforms will put you on their mailing list if you simply request It. It's not necessary to subscribe. These newsletters will generally update you on new acquisitions, listings of their most popular movies, and the latest news. Here are a few to consider: Netflix Life (netflixlife.com), Prime Insider Newsletter (amazon.com/primeinsider/newsletter), Apple Newsletter (mynews.apple.com/subscribe), HBOWatch (hbowatch.com), MHz Choice (mhzchoice.com/newsletter), FilmStruck (filmstruck.com), FX Newsletter (fxnetworks.com/newsletter), and the Roku Guide (rokuguide.com).

Books

These books are available on either Kindle, in hardcover, or in paperback. All can be purchased on Amazon.

- ***"Streaming: Movies, Media, and Instant Access"*** by Wheeler Winston Dixon. Film stocks are vanishing, but the iconic images of the silver screen remain. A complete guide describing the transformation of the film industry.

- ***"Streaming Devices + Streaming Services"*** by Ken Wickham. This guide helps you set up your television to receive streaming content. It also features three charts comparing more than twenty devices.

- ***"Streaming, Sharing, Stealing: Big Data and the Future of Entertainment"*** by Michael D. Smith and Rahul Telang. Explores how big data is transforming the creative industries and how those industries can use lessons from Netflix, Amazon, and Apple to fight back.

- ***"Over the Top: How the Internet Is (Slowly But Surely) Changing the Television Industry"*** by Alan Wolk. Explains how the television industry is adapting to the digital era.

Conclusion

By all means take advantage of these free subscriptions. Benjamin Franklin hit the nail on the head when he said, "*An investment in knowledge pays the best interest.*"

William Gillette "Sherlock Holmes"
May 15th 1916

Glossary

Acorn TV. For a monthly or an annual fee, this subscription platform allows viewers to access all the available content in the platform's library.

ADC (analog-to-digital converter). A device that converts analog signals to digital signals.

Alexa. Amazon's virtual assistant that allows you to verbally communicate with your TV and other digital devices.

Amazon Fire TV. A media streaming unit, which when added to a TV, allows viewers to stream content from internet platforms like Netflix, Amazon, and iTunes, directly to the TV.

Amazon Instant Video. A transactional platform requiring you to pay for each film or series you access.

Amazon Prime. For a monthly or an annual fee, this subscription platform allows viewers to access all the available content in the platform's library.

Android TV. A version of the Android operating system primarily for digital media players such as TV sets, tablets, and computers. It's an operating system that features a user interface designed around content discovery and voice search.

Apple TV. A media streaming unit added to a TV set that allows viewers to stream content from internet platforms like Netflix, Amazon, and iTunes, directly to the TV.

AVOD (advertising-supported video on demand). The inclusion of advertising permits the site to stream content at no cost.

Bandwidth. Refers to the volume of information per unit that an internet connection can handle. Bandwidth is usually expressed as "bits per second", also known as Mbps. 60 Mbps is defined as data transfer at the rate of 60 million bits (megabits) every second.

Big Five Glories. A platform offering films in the public domain.

Bitrate. The amount of data that travels to your home every second.

Bluetooth. A wireless technology that allows transmitting data over short distances from fixed and mobile devices, and personal area networks. It was originally conceived as a wireless alternative to data cables.

Broadband. As it relates to the internet, it refers to information and content streaming that is faster than the dial-up type of internet connection.

Buffering. The stuttering and freezing of the picture. It usually occurs when packets (individual units of video) move through numerous routers from the source to the destination.

CBS All Access. For a monthly fee, this subscription platform allows the viewer to access all the content in the platform's library.

Chromecast. A media streaming unit added to a TV set that allows viewers to stream content from internet platforms like Netflix, Amazon, and iTunes, directly to the TV.

Classic Cinema. A platform that allows viewers free access to all the films in the platform's library without any advertising.

Classic Movies EZ. A platform offering films in the public domain.

CMoviesHD. A platform that allows viewers free access to all films in the platform's library without any advertising.

Crackle. An ad-supported platform that allows viewers free access to all the content in the platform's library.

Criterion Collection. An organization that collects and restores classic films. FilmStruck and Kanopy now offer films from the Criterion Collection.

Crunchyroll. For a monthly or an annual fee, this subscription platform allows viewers to access all the available content in the platform's library.

Curiosity Steaming. For a monthly or an annual fee, this subscription platform allows viewers to access all the available content in the platform's library.

Digitizing. Converting analog video and/or audio to digital.

DLNA (Digital Living Network Alliance). This device can access such content as movies and videos from other devices on the same network.

Dolby Vision. A premium, proprietary version of HDR with enhanced brightness and quality of the picture.

Downloading. Waiting for the film to be transferred to your device before you can watch it.

DTS (dedicated to sound). Chief competitor to Dolby Digital. DTS offers a simulated surround sound.

Ethernet. A "communications protocol" that works through a cable. It's used to wire digital networks and to connect them to TV and video devices.

4K Streaming. Often called 4K resolution or simply 4K, it refers to a horizontal screen display resolution of 4,000 pixels. It is now pretty standard on most smart TVs. Coming soon: 5K.

Fandango Now. A transactional platform requiring you to pay for each film you access.

FilmStruck. For a monthly or an annual fee, this subscription platform allows viewers to access all the available films in the platform's library.

Google Now. Google's virtual assistant that allows you to verbally communicate with your TV and other digital devices.

HBO GO. A platform available for no extra charge, but only for subscribers to one of HBO's cable or satellite services. HBO GO viewers are able to access the same HBO content offered on HBO NOW.

HBO NOW. For a monthly or an annual fee, this subscription platform allows viewers to access all the available content in the platform's library.

HDMI (high definition multimedia interface). An audiovisual interface for transmitting uncompressed video and/or audio to a compatible digital device.

HDR (high dynamic range). Available on most mid-range and high-end TVs. Enhances the contrast ratio (the brightness and darkness of the picture) and color accuracy.

HDR10. Created by Samsung to compete with HDR.

HDTV (high definition TV). Digital television producing 720 or 1080 progressively-scanned lines of video. Can be indicated as 720p, 1080i, or 1080p.

Hertz (Hz). The standard unit that measures sound and light wave speed per second. The ideal is now 120Hz for the 4K UHD TVs.

HFR (high frame rate). Refers to a frame rate higher than the usual 24-frames-per-second rate, resulting in a smoother playback.

Hoopla. A platform that allows viewers free access to all content in the platform's library without any advertising.

Hulu Plus. For a monthly or an annual fee, this subscription platform allows viewers to access all the content in the platform's library.

Internet. A global system of interconnected computer networks that link to worldwide network devices such as the ones in your home.

Internet Archive. A platform that allows viewers free access to all the content in the platform's library without any advertising.

iOS. A mobile operating system developed by Apple to run the iPhone, iPad, and iPod touch. Originally known as the iPhone OS, the name was changed with the introduction of the iPad. It's the core software that's loaded on all Apple devices to allow them to run and support the many available apps.

ISP (internet service provider). A company that provides services for accessing the internet.

iTunes. A platform that does not require a subscription but charges viewers for each video or audio file that is accessed.

Kanopy. A platform that allows viewers free access to all the films in the platform's library without any advertising.

kHz (kilohertz). A unit of frequency. One kilohertz is equal to 1,000 hertz, which is 1,000 cycles per second.

LCD (liquid crystal display). A flat-panel display that uses the light-modulating properties of liquid crystals.

LED (light-emitting diode). A semiconductor light source that emits light when activated.

Live Video Streaming. The process of transmitting events in real time, over the internet, directly to viewers. Common examples are sporting events, concerts, theatrical shows, lectures, and religious services.

Media Streamer. A separate unit attached to or inserted into the TV that will allow viewers to stream multiple internet platforms like Netflix, Amazon, and iTunes, directly to the TV.

Megabites. A measure of computer memory or storage.

MLBTV. For a set fee (usually for the season) you can stream major league baseball games both current and past.

Modem. It serves as the bridge between the devices in your home and the Internet.

MUBI. For a monthly or an annual fee, this subscription platform allows viewers to access all the available films in the platform's library.

Netflix. For a monthly or an annual fee, this subscription platform allows viewers to access all the available content in the platform's library.

NFC (near field communication). Enables two electronic devices, such as a smartphone and a TV, to communicate with each other.

OLED/OLED HDR (organic light-emitting diode). A new technology developed by LG. It produces darker blacks, thus enhancing dark scenes and providing excellent color reproduction. It also offers wider viewing angles. Works best in well-lit rooms and for when many people in the room are watching the TV from different angles.

Open Culture Films. A platform offering films in the public domain.

OTT (over-the-top). The delivery of film, audio, or media content through the internet without requiring viewers to subscribe to a cable or satellite pay service like Comcast or Cablevision.

Paramount Movies. A platform that does not require a subscription but that charges viewers for each film that is accessed.

Pixel. The most basic unit of an image displayed on a video screen. The number of pixels determine the degree of brightness and colors on a TV screen.

Platforms, Digital. Refers to content providers such as Netflix, Amazon, and iTunes.

Popcornflix.com. A free platform with no advertising and a variety of genres including many movies for kids.

Popcornflix.site. A platform that allows viewers free access to all the films in the platform's library mostly without any advertising.

QLED (quantum light-emitting diode). With a QLED TV, the quantum dots are contained on a type of film, and the light that hits them is provided by an LED backlight. That light then travels through a liquid crystal display (LCD) layer to create a brighter picture.

Redbox on Demand. A platform that does not require a subscription, but that charges viewers for each film that is accessed.

Resolution. The number of pixels that compose the picture on the TV.

Roku/Roku Ultra. These are media streamer units added to a TV set that will allow viewers to stream content from internet outlets like Netflix, Amazon, and iTunes, directly to the TV.

Roku Channel. An ad-supported platform that allows viewers free access to all the films in the platform's library.

Router. A device that connects and routes the devices in your home or office. It performs the traffic-directing functions of the Internet.

SDTV (standard definition television). This is a television system that uses a resolution lower than 720p.

Showtime Anytime. For a monthly or an annual fee, this subscription platform allows viewers to access all the available content in the platform's library.

Siri. Apple's virtual assistant that allows you to verbally communicate with your TV and other digital devices.

Smart TV. A TV capable of direct internet connectivity that will allow it to stream multiple platforms.

SnagFilms. An ad-supported platform that allows viewers free access to all the films in the platform's library.

Sound Bar. A unit attached to the TV to enhance sound quality and volume.

Sound Base. Similar to a sound bar, except, as a space saver, it is placed underneath the TV.

Streaming Video. Content (such as video) that can be played directly through the internet to the viewing screen.

Subwoofer. A loudspeaker that enhances the low-pitched sounds, such as in the bass and sub-bass audio ranges.

SVOD. (subscription video on demand). For a set monthly or annual fee, a viewer is permitted to access all the available content in a platform's library.

TCM. (Turner Classic Movies). A cable channel that features films from the Turner Entertainment film library, films from Warner Bros. (released before 1950), and Metro-Goldwyn-Mayer (released before 1986). TCM films can now also be streamed on the FilmStruck platform.

The Video Cellar. A platform offering film in the public domain.

Tubi TV. An ad-supported platform that allows viewers free access to all the content in the platform's library.

TVOD (transactional video on demand). You pay each time you view a film or other video product. There is no monthly subscription cost.

UHD (ultra high definition). UHD is now standard with most 4K television sets.

UltraViolet. Allows you to add the movies you purchase to your cloud based online ultraviolet library, at no cost, and to then instantly stream and download the content to a wide variety of devices.

Uncle Earl's Classic Television. A platform offering films in the public domain.

USB (universal serial bus). One of the types of wire connectors that allow hook up of peripheral devices to computers and TV sets.

Viewster. A platform that allows viewers free access to all the films in the platform's library without any advertising.

VOD (video on demand). Content that can be viewed, on demand, by the viewer.

Vudu. An ad-supported platform that allows viewers free access to all the content in the platform's library.

Watch Documentaries. An ad-supported platform that allows viewers free access to all the films in the platform's library.

Wi-Fi (wireless fidelity). Uses radio frequencies to send signals to such devices as personal computers, smartphones, tablets, and smart TVs. It also provides internet access to devices within its wireless network.

WPS (Wi-Fi protected setup). Eliminates the need to manually enter a password. You're connected by simply pressing a button on the router and another button on the device.

XUMO. An ad-supported platform that allows viewers free access to all the content in the platform's library.

My Thanks

This book could not have been written without the able assistance of Scott Prater. His work in fact-checking every entry, editing the material, organizing the overall text, and his numerous suggestions throughout the book-writing process, were invaluable.